Norse Mythology

A Collection of the Best Norse Myths

Jason Dodd

Table of Contents

Introduction

Welcome to "Norse Mythology: A Collection of the Best Norse Myths," a journey into the heart of ancient Nordic tales, where gods, giants, and mortals play out their roles against the backdrop of a cosmos both vast and intricate. This book is a gateway to a world where the boundaries between myth and reality blur, where the forces of nature and the whims of deities intertwine to weave the rich tapestry of Norse legend.

In the shadowy realms of Norse mythology, the universe is alive with a pantheon of deities, each embodying aspects of life and nature. The first chapter of this book, 'The Aesir and Vanir,' introduces you to these celestial beings. Here, you will meet the Aesir gods, known for their warrior nature and ties to power and conquest, and the Vanir gods, associated with fertility, wisdom, and foresight. This chapter delves into their origins, their powers, and the intricate relationships that define their existence.

Chapter 2, 'Other Characters,' broadens the scope of our exploration to include the myriad beings that populate these myths. From the mighty giants who often stand in opposition to the gods, to the enigmatic valkyries, the crafty dwarves, and other creatures, this chapter paints a vivid picture of the diverse inhabitants of the Norse cosmos.

Subsequent chapters are dedicated to the most compelling stories from Norse mythology. Chapter 3, 'Creation Myth,' narrates the astonishing birth of the cosmos, an event that sets the stage for the sagas that follow. 'The Aesir-Vanir War' in Chapter 4 recounts the epic conflict and eventual reconciliation between the two divine tribes, a tale that echoes the themes of strife and unity.

In Chapter 5, we encounter 'The Binding of Fenrir,' a story that illustrates the complex relationship between fate and free will. 'The Theft of Thor's Hammer' in Chapter 6 reveals a blend of might and cunning, showcasing the depth of the characters involved. Chapter 7, 'Odin and the Mead of Poetry,' explores the quest for wisdom and the origins of poetic inspiration.

Chapter 8, 'The Fortification of Asgard,' tells of the gods' efforts to protect their realm, a narrative filled with trickery and craftsmanship. The tragic 'Death of Baldur,' presented in Chapter 9, plunges the reader into a tale of prophecy, loss, and the inevitability of fate. Finally, Chapter 10, 'Ragnarök,' culminates in the ultimate destiny of the gods—a tale of destruction, rebirth, and the enduring cycle of life.

As you turn these pages, you will be transported to a world where magic and mystery reign, where the clash of swords and the whisper of prophecy echo, and where each story is a thread in the grand tapestry of Norse mythology. This collection is not just a recounting of myths but an invitation to wander through a realm that has captivated the human imagination for centuries.

In conclusion, these stories, more than mere tales of gods and monsters, are reflections of the human spirit, its struggles, triumphs, and the perpetual quest for understanding the mysteries of life and the universe. Prepare to embark on a journey through time and legend, a journey that promises to enchant, enlighten, and inspire.

Chapter 1: The Aesir and Vanir

The Aesir and Vanir are two distinct groups of gods and goddesses in Norse mythology, each with their own unique characteristics and domains.

The **Aesir** are primarily associated with power, war, and governance. They reside in Asgard, one of the nine worlds connected by the cosmic tree, Yggdrasil. The Aesir are often involved in complex interactions with other beings, including the Vanir and various giants, and their narratives frequently revolve around themes of conflict, heroism, and the pursuit of knowledge and power.

The **Vanir**, on the other hand, are closely linked to fertility, agriculture, wealth, and nature. They are typically depicted as wiser and more peaceful, often serving as gods of prosperity and worldly well-being. The Vanir reside in Vanaheim, another of the nine worlds.

The existence of these two separate groups of deities reflects the diverse aspects of life and society in ancient Norse culture. Initially, the Aesir and Vanir were in conflict with each other, as depicted in the Aesir-Vanir War (more on this in chapter 4). This war ultimately ended in a truce, with an exchange of hostages leading to greater unity and cooperation between the two groups.

In this opening chapter, we will introduce you to these fascinating Gods and Goddesses.

The Aesir

Odin

In Norse mythology, Odin is a principal deity, revered as the god of wisdom, war, death, magic, poetry, and prophecy. As the Allfather and the chief of the Aesir gods, he rules over Asgard, the realm of the gods. Odin is depicted as a complex, multifaceted figure, embodying both the warlike aspects of a warrior king and the deep wisdom of a sage. He is often portrayed as a wanderer, a seeker of knowledge, willing to sacrifice for greater understanding, including the famous myth where he sacrifices one of his eyes at Mimir's well for wisdom.

Odin's role in Norse mythology is vast and varied. He is a god who relentlessly pursues knowledge, even at great personal cost, and is associated with magic, particularly the runes and seidr, a form of Norse magic. He is also the god who brings the slain warriors, chosen by his Valkyries, to Valhalla, his hall in Asgard, where they become Einherjar, warriors who prepare for Ragnarök, the end of the world. Odin's connection to death is not merely as a war deity but also as a psychopomp, guiding souls to the afterlife.

His character is marked by a profound sense of the tragic and the inevitability of fate, often reflected in his quest to find a way to avoid Ragnarök, despite knowing that it is unpreventable. Odin is also a figure of poetic inspiration, credited with discovering the runes, which, in addition to being an alphabet, were also magical symbols. His two ravens, Huginn (thought) and Muninn (memory), fly across the world daily and bring back news to him, symbolizing his far-reaching knowledge and wisdom.

In Norse myths, Odin is often engaged in gaining knowledge, sometimes even engaging in deception or manipulation to achieve his goals, which reflects the Norse value of cunning and strategic thinking. His complex nature, embodying wisdom, war, and magic, makes him one of the most interesting and important figures in Norse mythology.

Thor

Thor is the god of thunder, lightning, storms, oak trees, strength, the protection of mankind, and also hallowing and fertility. He is the son of Odin, the chief of the Aesir gods, and Fjörgyn, a personification of the earth. Thor is most famous for his mighty hammer, Mjolnir, a magical weapon that returns to him after being thrown and is capable of leveling mountains. He is also known for his incredible physical strength, bravery, and his role as a protector of Asgard and Midgard (the realm of humans).

Thor's role in Norse mythology is that of a formidable warrior and a guardian against the forces of chaos and destruction, often represented by giants (jötnar). He is frequently depicted battling these giants, preventing them from causing harm to the gods and humans. Thor's confrontations with the Midgard Serpent, Jormungandr, are particularly notable; their final battle is prophesied to occur during Ragnarök, the end of the world. Despite his fierce demeanor in battle, Thor is also revered as a deity of the common man, being especially popular among farmers and warriors. He was invoked for protection, strength, and fertility.

Thor's character is marked by more than just physical prowess; he is also known for his straightforwardness and his unwavering sense of duty. Unlike Odin, who is characterized by his cunning and strategic mind, Thor is more direct in his approach, often resorting to physical solutions over diplomatic or cunning ones. This straightforwardness made him relatable and revered among the Norse people. Thor's adventures, often involving his travels and battles, are some of the most popular tales in Norse mythology, reflecting the values of strength, courage, and protection against the adversities of life.

Frigg

Frigg is a prominent goddess, renowned as the wife of Odin and the queen of the Aesir gods. She is primarily associated with marriage, motherhood, fertility, love, household management, and domestic arts. Frigg holds a position of high esteem and authority in Asgard, the realm of the gods, and is often depicted as a figure of dignity and foreknowledge.

As a goddess, Frigg's role extends beyond her marital and maternal aspects. She is known for her ability to foresee the future, although she does not reveal what she knows.

Frigg's personality is characterized by her wisdom, foresight, and her caring, protective nature over her family and the Aesir gods. She is often portrayed as a loving and devoted wife and mother, embodying the ideal matronly figure. Frigg's presence in Norse mythology symbolizes the importance of the family unit, the sanctity of marriage, and the nurturing aspect of motherhood within the Norse social structure.

In addition to her familial roles, Frigg is sometimes involved in matters of governance and decision-making in Asgard, often advising Odin. Her name is thought to be the origin of the English word "Friday" (akin to "Frigg's day"), reflecting her significant cultural and religious influence in the Norse world.

Sif

Sif, in Norse mythology, is a goddess associated primarily with earth, fertility, and family. She is best known as the wife of Thor, the mighty god of thunder, which positions her as an important figure in the Aesir pantheon. Sif is depicted as a symbol of fertility and familial harmony, embodying the nurturing aspect of the earth.

One of the most famous myths involving Sif is the story of her golden hair. Sif was renowned for her beautiful, long golden hair, often interpreted as a symbol of golden wheat fields and hence fertility and abundance. In a mischievous and malevolent act, Loki, the trickster god, cuts off Sif's hair, leaving her bald. This act angers Thor, who threatens Loki, forcing him to make amends. Loki then commissions the dwarves, skilled craftsmen of the gods, to create new hair for Sif made of gold. This hair, imbued with magical properties, grows like natural hair and restores Sif's beauty and symbolizes the renewal and resilience of nature.

Apart from this tale, Sif does not feature prominently in the surviving Norse myths, but her role as Thor's wife and her association with the earth and fertility are significant. In a culture deeply connected to agriculture and the natural world, Sif's representation of the earth's fertility would have been of considerable importance. She embodies the ideal of the nurturing mother and caretaker, contributing to the well-being and sustenance of both gods and humans.

Tyr

Tyr is a god of war and justice, known for his bravery, law-giving, and crucial role in maintaining order and fairness. While his exact lineage is somewhat ambiguous, he is often considered a son of Odin, the chief god. In the earlier Germanic and Norse traditions, Tyr was a highly esteemed deity, sometimes even regarded as the chief god before Odin's prominence in the Viking Age.

Tyr's most famous mythological tale is his involvement in the binding of Fenrir, the monstrous wolf and a son of Loki (this story is covered in detail in chapter 5).

Tyr's role in Norse mythology extends beyond the tale of Fenrir. He is often associated with law and order, and his name is believed to be related to the Old Norse word for "god" and the Old English word "tiw," associated with "Tiwesdaeg" (Tuesday). In the Norse pantheon, Tyr is not as prominent as Odin or Thor but is revered for his bravery and importance in maintaining the cosmic balance of justice and order.

Baldur

Baldur, in Norse mythology, is a beloved god known for his beauty, grace, and fairness. He is the son of Odin, the chief of the Aesir gods, and Frigg, the goddess of marriage and motherhood. Baldur is often portrayed as a figure of light and purity, embodying the best of the divine characteristics. His death is one of the most significant and poignant tales in Norse mythology and is seen as a precursor to the cataclysmic event of Ragnarök, the end of the world.

Baldur's role in Norse mythology is often interpreted symbolically; he is seen as the personification of innocence, beauty, and goodness. His death represents the loss of these ideal qualities from the world and signifies the onset of a darker, more tumultuous era. In the myths, Baldur's character does not take on aggressive or warlike traits like many other Norse gods but instead embodies a sense of peace and benevolence.

Heimdallr

Heimdallr, or Heimdall, is a unique and enigmatic deity, often depicted as a guardian and watchman of the gods. His primary role is as the sentinel of Bifrost, the rainbow bridge that connects Asgard, the realm of the gods, to Midgard, the world of humanity. Heimdallr is known for his extraordinary senses;

he can hear wool growing on sheep, and he can see for hundreds of leagues. He is also said to require less sleep than a bird.

Heimdallr's origins are somewhat mysterious, with different sources providing varying accounts. He is often described as the son of nine mothers, who may be personifications of the waves, and is sometimes considered to be of noble birth, possibly even a son of Odin. His most famous possession is the Gjallarhorn, a powerful horn that he will blow to signal the onset of Ragnarok, the end of the world as foretold in Norse prophecy.

One of Heimdallr's key narratives involves his role in the events leading to Ragnarok. He is destined to sound the Gjallarhorn to alert the Aesir to the final battle, where he will face and eventually slay Loki, but will also be mortally wounded in the encounter.

Heimdallr's role as a guardian extends beyond the physical protection of Asgard. He is also seen as a protector of the social order and the moral rectitude of gods and men. Some myths also credit him with creating the social classes among humanity. His vigilant nature and unwavering dedication to his duty as a guardian make him a symbol of watchfulness and preparedness, embodying the Norse value of vigilance in the face of impending chaos and conflict.

Bragi

Bragi is a unique deity in Norse mythology, revered as the god of poetry, music, and eloquence. He is often portrayed as a wise and eloquent figure, with a long beard, and is associated with skaldic poetry, a form of court poetry that originated in Scandinavia. Bragi's role in Norse mythological tales is less about physical prowess or magical feats and more about the art of words and their power.

According to some accounts, Bragi is said to be a son of Odin, the chief of the Aesir gods. However, other sources suggest that he may have been a historical poet whose legends and prowess were so great that over time, he was deified in the Norse pantheon. This blending of historical and mythological narratives is not uncommon in ancient mythologies.

In the halls of Asgard, the realm of the gods, Bragi occupies a vital role as the bard, regaling gods and fallen warriors in Valhalla with his stories and poems. His eloquence is not merely entertainment but also a symbol of the cultural and intellectual aspects of Norse society. He is married to Idunn, the goddess of youth and rejuvenation.

Bragi's presence in Norse mythology highlights the importance and reverence for the spoken word and poetry in Norse culture. Skalds, the poets of the Norse world, were highly regarded, and Bragi's character embodies this respect and admiration.

Idunn

Idunn is a significant goddess in Norse mythology, primarily known for her role as the keeper of the magical apples that grant the gods eternal youth and vitality. She is often depicted as a symbol of rejuvenation and spring, embodying the renewal of life. Idunn is married to Bragi, the god of poetry, and her presence in Asgard, the realm of the gods, is crucial for maintaining the gods' immortality and vigor.

Idunn's character is not marked by the warrior-like traits or political intrigues common to other Norse deities. Instead, she represents the nurturing aspect of nature, the gentle but essential force that sustains and rejuvenates life. Her role as the guardian of the apples symbolizes the Norse understanding of youth and life's cyclic nature – themes that are vital in a culture that often faced harsh natural conditions and valued resilience and renewal.

Hodr

Hodr, sometimes spelled Höðr, is a somewhat tragic figure in Norse mythology, known primarily for his role in the death of his brother, Baldur (this myth is covered in chapter 9). Hodr is typically depicted as the blind god, a son of Odin and Frigg, and his story is deeply intertwined with the themes of fate and tragedy that are prevalent in Norse myths.

The character of Hodr in Norse mythology, though not as elaborately detailed as some other gods, embodies the themes of innocence, manipulation, and the inexorable nature of fate. His story is a poignant example of how the Norse myths often explore the complexities of fate and destiny, where even the gods are not immune to the predetermined course of events.

Vidar

Vidar is a somewhat enigmatic yet powerful figure in Norse mythology, often described as the son of Odin, the chief of the Aesir gods, and the giantess Gridr. He is known as the "Silent God," a deity of few words but immense strength, often characterized as a god of vengeance and resilience.

One of Vidar's most defining characteristics is his strong, thick shoe, which plays a crucial role in his mythology. This shoe is made from all the scraps of leather that people have cut from the toes and heels of their shoes throughout time, symbolizing the collective effort and sacrifice. Vidar's shoe is essential for his destiny during Ragnarök, the end of the world in Norse mythology.

Vidar's most significant role comes during Ragnarök, where he avenges his father Odin's death. According to the prophecies, after Odin is devoured by the wolf Fenrir, Vidar will step forward to slay the wolf. He does so by using his formidable shoe to hold open the beast's jaws and then ripping them apart, thus avenging Odin and demonstrating his incredible strength. This act of vengeance against Fenrir makes Vidar one of the few gods prophesied to survive Ragnarök, along with a small number of other gods who will rebuild the new world.

In Norse mythology, Vidar is often associated with the virtues of stoicism and strength in the face of adversity. He is not a god of conquest or glory in battle, like Thor or Odin, but rather a symbol of enduring strength and the capacity for vengeance when necessary.

Váli

Váli is a lesser-known but significant figure in Norse mythology, often depicted as a god of vengeance. His origins are unique; he is born expressly for the purpose of avenging the death of Baldur, one of the most beloved gods, who was killed by the blind god Hodr under the influence of the trickster Loki. Váli is usually described as a son of Odin, the chief god, and the giantess Rindr, and his birth is characterized by rapid growth and development – he matures to full adulthood within a very short time, emphasizing his role as an avenger.

The central myth involving Váli is his role in avenging Baldur's death. As soon as he is born, Váli sets out to fulfill this purpose. He kills Hodr, thus avenging his half-brother Baldur. This act of retribution is significant in Norse mythology, as it represents the swift and unrelenting nature of vengeance in accordance with Norse values. In some versions of the myth, Váli also plays a role in punishing Loki for his part in Baldur's death.

Váli's character is primarily defined by this singular purpose. Unlike many Norse gods who have various adventures and complex narratives, Váli's existence is largely centered around the act of vengeance. He is one of the few gods prophesied to survive Ragnarök, the great battle at the end of the world.

Ullr

Ullr, in Norse mythology, is a somewhat mysterious and lesser-known deity, often associated with archery, skiing, hunting, and winter. His name is thought to be derived from a word meaning "glory" or "splendor," which reflects his status as a skilled and respected god. Ullr is traditionally considered a son of Sif and a stepson of Thor, though some sources suggest other parentage.

While the myths about Ullr are not as plentiful or detailed as those of other Norse gods, he is depicted as a skilled warrior and hunter, possessing an exceptional prowess in archery and skiing. This makes him particularly important during the winter months, where his skills are most advantageous. Ullr is believed to be a god who can traverse the snow-covered lands with ease and grace, and he is often invoked for success in hunting and in personal combat.

Ullr's role also extends to that of an oath-god, where solemn oaths are sworn over rings in his name. This aspect of his character underscores his association with law and order, and the importance of keeping one's word, which was a highly valued trait in Norse society.

In terms of worship and representation, Ullr was likely a significant deity in the early Norse pantheon, especially in regions with harsh winters. Archaeological evidence, such as place names and inscriptions, suggests that he was widely revered. However, over time, his prominence seems to have waned, leading to a scarcity of detailed stories about him in surviving Norse mythology.

Forseti

Forseti is a Norse god of justice, peace, and fair judgement, though he is not as widely known as other deities like Odin or Thor. He is the son of Baldur, the god of light and purity, which aligns him with some of the more benevolent aspects of the Norse pantheon. Forseti is often depicted as a wise and eloquent arbitrator, whose primary role is to settle disputes and maintain harmony among the gods and humans.

In Norse mythology, Forseti resides in Glitnir, his hall in Asgard, which is described as a radiant place of peace and fairness. Glitnir, whose name means "Glistening," is said to have a silver roof and golden pillars, symbolizing the light of truth and the value of justice. Here, Forseti presides over legal disputes, offering resolutions that are always just and accepted by all parties. His ability to find peaceful solutions and his unwavering commitment to fairness earn him the respect and trust of both gods and mortals.

There are not many myths specifically detailing Forseti's adventures or exploits, unlike other Norse gods. His character is more symbolic, representing the ideal of justice and the importance of lawful and fair resolution in conflicts.

The Vanir

Njord

Njord, in Norse mythology, is a prominent deity associated with the sea, wind, fishing, wealth, and fertility. He is a member of the Vanir, a group of gods associated with nature, fertility, and prosperity, and becomes an important figure among the Aesir following the Aesir-Vanir War and the subsequent exchange of hostages for peace.

Njord is often depicted as a god who brings wealth and prosperity to those on land and at sea, making him particularly important to sailors, fishermen, and coastal dwellers. As the father of Freyr and Freyja, two other significant deities associated with fertility and prosperity, his influence extends across several key aspects of life in the Norse world.

Njord's role as a sea deity is significant in Norse culture, which placed a high value on seafaring and maritime activities. He embodies the essential qualities of the sea: its power to both give and take away, its role in trade and travel, and its influence on the fertility and prosperity of the land.

Freyja

Freyja, in Norse mythology, is a prominent and powerful goddess, renowned for her associations with love, beauty, fertility, war, and magic. She is a member of the Vanir, the group of gods known for their connection to nature and fertility, and she becomes an integral part of the Aesir gods following the Aesir-Vanir War. Freyja is the daughter of Njord, the sea god, and the sister of Freyr, another important fertility god.

Freyja is a multifaceted deity, embodying both the nurturing aspects of love and fertility, as well as the more severe elements of war and death. She is said to ride a chariot pulled by cats, and she possesses a feathered cloak that allows her to fly in the form of a falcon. One of her most notable attributes is her necklace Brísingamen, crafted by dwarves, which symbolizes her beauty and power.

In terms of her role in the afterlife, Freyja is unique. Half of the warriors who die in battle are claimed by her (the other half go to Odin's hall, Valhalla), and they are brought to her realm, Fólkvangr, a field of the afterlife where the warriors are honored. This aspect of her character ties her to the Valkyries, the choosers of the slain, and highlights her dual role as a goddess of both life and death.

Freyja is also deeply associated with the practice of seidr, a form of Norse magic concerned with discerning and altering the course of destiny. As a practitioner of seidr, she is a figure of great mystical power and knowledge. Her involvement in these magical practices further cements her status as a goddess of great complexity and influence.

Freyr

Freyr, a prominent and widely revered god in Norse mythology, is associated with fertility, prosperity, peace, and good weather. As a member of the Vanir, a group of gods connected with fertility, nature, and prosperity, Freyr plays a significant role in Norse mythological narratives. He is the son of the sea god Njord and the brother of Freyja, the goddess of love and fertility, making him part of a divine family deeply involved in matters of growth and abundance.

Freyr is often depicted as a benevolent and generous god, bringing good fortune and wealth to those who honor him. He is particularly venerated for his control over the rain and sunshine, essential elements for successful agriculture. This connection to the growth and fertility of the earth makes him an essential deity for farmers and rural communities in the Norse world.

Freyr also possesses several magical items, including a ship that can be folded up and carried in a pouch, and a boar with bristles that shine in the dark, both symbolizing abundance and wealth.

In Norse mythology, Freyr's character embodies the prosperity of the land and the well-being of its people. He represents the life-giving aspects of nature and the importance of harmony between the environment and society. Freyr's worship and mythology reflect the Norse people's understanding of and dependence on the natural world's cycles and their reverence for the divine forces governing these elements.

Kvasir

Kvasir in Norse mythology is a unique and wise being, born from the saliva of the Aesir and Vanir gods. According to the myth, after the war between the Aesir and Vanir ended, both sides spat into a jar as a symbol of peace. From this saliva, Kvasir was created, embodying the combined wisdom and knowledge of both groups of gods. He is considered the wisest of all beings and is often depicted as a traveling teacher who shares his knowledge freely across the world.

Kvasir's role in Norse mythology is primarily associated with the story of the creation of the Mead of Poetry, a substance that bestows the gift of poetry and wisdom upon those who drink it. In the myth, Kvasir is killed by two dwarves, Fjalar and Galar, who were envious of his wisdom. The dwarves mix his blood with honey, creating the Mead of Poetry. This mead is subsequently stolen by the giant Suttungr, who hides it away. Odin, desiring the mead for its potent abilities, goes to great lengths to retrieve it, eventually succeeding and bringing it back to Asgard. The Mead of Poetry is thus considered to contain Kvasir's wisdom.

Kvasir's story, while not as action-packed as those of the gods like Thor or Odin, plays a crucial role in the Norse mythological narrative, underscoring the deep respect for wisdom and learning in Norse society and the complex interplay between knowledge, creativity, and the divine.

Chapter 2: Other Characters

In addition to the Aesir and Vanir deities, Norse mythology is host to a range of different characters, including other Gods and Goddesses, Giants, Monsters, and more. In this chapter, we will introduce you to some of the many characters that feature in the Norse myths.

Giants (Jötnar)

Ymir

Ymir is a primordial being and a central figure in Norse cosmogony, known as the progenitor of the race of giants (Jötnar) and an essential element in the creation myth of the Norse universe. In Norse mythology, Ymir is born from the interaction of the elemental forces of heat and cold. His origins lie in the Ginnungagap, the great void that existed before the world was created, situated between the realms of Niflheim (the land of ice) and Muspelheim (the land of fire). When the heat from Muspelheim met the ice of Niflheim in Ginnungagap, the melting ice drops gave life to Ymir.

Ymir is often depicted as a hermaphroditic entity who could reproduce asexually, and from him, the race of giants is said to have originated. According to the myths, as Ymir slept, he sweated, and from his sweat, the first male and female giants were born from under his left arm, and a six-headed giant grew from his legs.

The myth takes a significant turn when Ymir is killed by Odin and his brothers, Vili and Ve. From Ymir's dismembered body, the brothers fashion the world: his flesh becomes the earth, his blood the seas, his bones the mountains, his hair the trees, and his skull the sky. Even the clouds are said to be made from his brain matter, thrown into the sky by Odin and his brothers.

Ymir's role in Norse mythology is foundational. He is the ancestral figure from whom the first beings emerged, and his body is the material from which the cosmos is made. The act of creating the world from Ymir's body reflects a common theme in ancient mythologies, where the cosmos is formed from the body of a primordial being.

Loki

Loki is one of the most complex and controversial figures in Norse mythology, known for his cunning, shape-shifting abilities, and mischievous nature. Unlike many of the gods, Loki is not of divine origin. He is a Jötunn by birth, but through a blood pact, he becomes a sworn brother to Odin, the chief of the Aesir gods, and thus takes his place among them in Asgard. Loki's parentage and his dual affiliation with the gods and the

Jötnar contribute to his role as a trickster and a figure who often straddles the line between ally and adversary.

Loki is involved in numerous tales within Norse mythology, where his cunning, wit, and talent for deception are prominently displayed. He is often the catalyst for many of the challenges and problems faced by the gods, yet he is also the source of inventive solutions. One of his most famous exploits is his involvement in the construction of Asgard's walls, where he tricks a giant builder and ensures the gods keep their stronghold without paying the agreed price. Loki's shape-shifting ability allows him to take various forms, including that of a mare, which leads to the birth of Sleipnir, Odin's eight-legged horse.

Despite his contributions, Loki's actions are not always benign. His role becomes increasingly malevolent as the myths progress, culminating in his direct involvement in the death of Baldur, one of the most beloved of the Aesir gods. This act of malice sets into motion the events leading to Ragnarök, the prophesied end of the world. During Ragnarök, Loki sides against the gods, leading the forces of chaos and destruction in the final battle.

Surtr

Surtr is a formidable and fearsome figure, often associated with fire and destruction. He is a Jötunn and is primarily known for his pivotal role in Ragnarök, the prophesied end of the world. Surtr originates from Muspelheim, the fiery realm in Norse cosmology, and is described as being a ruler or guardian of this fiery land.

Surtr's most significant role is during Ragnarök, where he leads the forces of Muspelheim against the gods of Asgard. He is depicted wielding a flaming sword, so bright and hot that it shines and burns like the sun itself. In the cataclysmic events of Ragnarök, Surtr is prophesied to engage in a fierce battle against the gods, bringing about great destruction. It is foretold that he will set the world ablaze, engulfing the earth in fire, leading to its eventual destruction and renewal. In this apocalyptic scenario, Surtr plays the role of the ultimate destroyer, whose actions lead to the end of the old world order and pave the way for the creation of a new world from the ashes of the old.

Thrym

Thrym is a character from Norse mythology, known primarily as a king of the Jötnar. He is most famously depicted in the myth involving the theft of Thor's hammer, Mjolnir. Thrym's story is recounted in the "Þrymskviða" (The Lay of Thrym), which is part of the Poetic Edda, a collection of Old Norse poems from the medieval manuscript Codex Regius.

In the myth, Thrym steals Mjolnir, Thor's powerful hammer, and hides it deep within the earth. He demands Freyja, the goddess of love and beauty, as his bride in exchange for the return of the hammer. The gods, desperate to retrieve Mjolnir, which is vital for the defense of Asgard against the giants, concoct a plan. Thor, along with Loki, devises a scheme to trick Thrym. Thor dresses up as Freyja, with Loki as his bridesmaid, and they travel to Jotunheim, the land of the giants, to meet Thrym.

Thrym, deceived by the disguise, prepares for the wedding. However, he becomes suspicious due to "Freyja's" (Thor in disguise) voracious appetite and un-ladylike behavior. Loki, quick-witted, explains these oddities as signs of Freyja's excitement to marry Thrym. Finally, when Thrym brings out Mjolnir to bless the marriage, Thor reveals his true identity, regains his hammer, and uses it to defeat Thrym and the other giants present, thus saving Asgard.

Thrym's character in Norse mythology is typical of the Jötnar, often portrayed as antagonistic to the gods but not inherently evil. , with its playful narrative and the gods' use of disguise and deception.

Skadi

Skadi is a Jötunn and goddess, known for her associations with winter, skiing, hunting, and mountains. Her character is often depicted as strong, independent, and closely connected to the wild and untamed aspects of nature. Skadi is unique in the Norse pantheon as she transitions from her origins as a giantess to become a goddess, illustrating the complex relationships between the Aesir gods and the Jötnar.

The most well-known myth involving Skadi is related to the death of her father, Thjazi. Thjazi is killed by the gods after he kidnaps the goddess Idunn. Seeking vengeance for her father's death, Skadi arms herself and heads to Asgard, the realm of the gods. Instead of vengeance, however, a compromise is reached: Skadi is allowed to choose a husband from among the gods, but she must make her choice based only on their feet. Hoping to select the god Baldur, she instead chooses Njord, the sea god, because of his beautiful feet. This marriage symbolizes the union of opposites - Skadi, a lover of mountains and winter, and Njord, who prefers the sea and summer. Ultimately, their marriage fails due to their inability to agree on where to live.

Gerðr

Gerðr (often anglicized as Gerd) is a figure from Norse mythology, renowned for her unparalleled beauty and her role in a prominent love story with the god Freyr. Gerðr is a Jötunn or giantess, and her narrative is a classic example of the intertwining of the divine with the more elemental forces of the Norse cosmos.

Gerðr's most notable myth is detailed in the "Skírnismál," a part of the Poetic Edda. The story begins when Freyr, a god associated with fertility, prosperity, and peace, spies Gerðr in Jötunheimr, the land of the giants, from Odin's high seat, Hlidskjalf. Struck by her beauty, Freyr instantly falls in love and becomes deeply despondent when he realizes that she is beyond his reach, as the worlds of the Aesir gods and the giants are often in conflict.

To win Gerðr's affection, Freyr sends his servant Skirnir to Jötunheimr with gifts and promises of wealth. Gerðr, however, initially rejects these advances. It is only after Skirnir resorts to threats, invoking magic and curses, that she reluctantly agrees to meet Freyr. Their union is seen as a symbolic integration of the Vanir (Freyr's group of gods, associated with fertility and prosperity) with the elemental and primal forces of nature (represented by Gerðr as a giantess). This marriage thus symbolizes a harmonious balance between different aspects of the natural world.

Hrungnir

Hrungnir is a Jötunn, known for his immense strength and his confrontation with the god Thor. His story is most notably recounted in the Prose Edda, written by Snorri Sturluson, a medieval Icelandic historian and poet.

Hrungnir's tale begins when he, in a drunken state, enters Asgard, the realm of the gods. Initially, the gods are amused by his boasting and offer him hospitality. However, Hrungnir's behavior soon becomes belligerent, and he starts to pose a threat, claiming he will demolish Asgard and take the gods' wives back to Jotunheim, the land of the giants. Angered by his words, the gods call upon Thor to deal with Hrungnir. Thor challenges Hrungnir to a duel, which is to take place at the border of Asgard.

Hrungnir, known for being the strongest of all giants, prepares for the fight by having a special heart made from hard stone, with three sharp points, symbolizing his formidable nature. In addition to this, the giants create a clay giant named Mokkurkalfi, meant to aid Hrungnir, but it is so frightened by Thor that it is of little help. In the ensuing battle, Thor and Hrungnir engage in a fierce fight. Thor eventually kills Hrungnir, striking him on the head with his hammer, Mjolnir.

Angrboda

Angrboda is a Jötunn, known primarily for her significant role as the mother of some of the most fearsome beings in the Norse cosmology. Her name, Angrboda, means "Bringer of Sorrow" or "Herald of Grief," which is indicative of her association with ominous and destructive forces.

Angrboda is most notable for her union with Loki, the trickster god. From their relationship, three of the most formidable and tragic beings in Norse mythology are born: Fenrir, the great wolf; Jormungandr, the Midgard Serpent; and Hel, who becomes the ruler of the underworld realm of the same name. Each of these offspring plays a significant role in Norse myth, particularly in the events leading up to and including Ragnarok, the end of the world.

Angrboda's character is shrouded in mystery, and there is little detail about her in the surviving Norse texts. However, her presence and her progeny are pivotal in the mythology.

Monsters and Creatures

Jormungandr

Jormungandr, also known as the Midgard Serpent, is a colossal and formidable creature in Norse mythology. He is one of the three children of Loki, the trickster god, and the giantess Angrboda, making him a significant figure in the Norse cosmological narrative. Jormungandr's siblings are Fenrir, the giant wolf, and Hel, the ruler of the underworld realm named after her.

According to the myth, Jormungandr is cast into the ocean by Odin, the chief of the Aesir gods, due to prophecies that foretell danger from Loki's offspring. Jormungandr grows so large in the ocean that he is able to encircle the entire world of Midgard and grasp his own tail. This immense size and his position encircling the world have made him a symbol of the boundaries that enclose the known world, as well as the cyclical nature of the Norse universe.

Jormungandr's most famous role is in the prophecy of Ragnarök. It is foretold that during Ragnarök, he will release his tail and emerge from the ocean, causing massive waves and flooding the land. Jormungandr will then engage in a cataclysmic battle with Thor, the god of thunder. Their fight is one of the most epic confrontations in Norse mythology. Thor will succeed in killing Jormungandr but will only take nine steps afterward before succumbing to the serpent's deadly poison, highlighting the theme of mutual destruction that is prevalent in the Ragnarök prophecy.

Fenrir

Fenrir is a prominent and fearsome figure in Norse mythology, known as a giant wolf and one of the three children of Loki, the trickster god, and the giantess Angrboda. Fenrir's role in the Norse mythological narrative is significant, particularly in the context of Ragnarök.

From his birth, Fenrir was exceptionally large and strong, growing at an alarming rate. The gods, aware of a prophecy that Fenrir would play a major role in their downfall, attempted to control him. They raised Fenrir in Asgard, but as he grew, so did their fear. The gods decided to bind Fenrir to prevent him from causing destruction. However, Fenrir was incredibly strong and broke every chain they attempted to use. Eventually, the gods commissioned the dwarves to create Gleipnir, a magical, unbreakable ribbon to contain him.

Fenrir's binding is one of the key events leading up to Ragnarök. It is foretold that during Ragnarök, Fenrir will break free from his bonds and join the giants in their battle against the gods. In this apocalyptic battle, Fenrir will confront and ultimately kill Odin, the chief of the Aesir gods, before being killed by Odin's son, Víðarr.

Ratatoskr

Ratatoskr is a unique and intriguing character in Norse mythology, known not for his might or magical powers, but for his role as a messenger and instigator. Ratatoskr is a squirrel whose primary function is to run up and down Yggdrasil, the world tree, carrying messages between the eagle perched atop Yggdrasil and Nidhogg, the dragon that dwells beneath one of the tree's three roots, gnawing at it.

This constant back-and-forth is more than just communication; Ratatoskr is often depicted as a gossip or troublemaker, conveying insults and stirring conflict between the eagle and the dragon. This role is symbolic, representing the continual strife and tension present in the world. The eagle and Nidhogg are often interpreted as embodying opposing cosmic forces or elements, and Ratatoskr's actions in exacerbating their rivalry symbolize the ongoing dynamic of conflict and balance in the cosmos.

Sleipnir

Sleipnir is a remarkable and extraordinary figure, renowned as the eight-legged horse ridden by Odin, the chief of the Aesir gods. Sleipnir is not just any steed but is considered the best of all horses, embodying speed, agility, and endurance. His unique eight-legged form grants him unparalleled stability and swiftness, making him capable of traversing great distances, including journeys between different realms of the Norse cosmos.

The origins of Sleipnir are as intriguing as his abilities. He is the offspring of the god Loki and the giant builder's horse, Svadilfari. According to the myth, the gods contract a giant, disguised as a builder, to construct a wall around Asgard, promising him the sun, the moon, and the goddess Freyja if he completes it within a single winter. To hasten the construction, the builder uses his powerful horse, Svadilfari. Loki, in the form of a mare, lures Svadilfari away to sabotage the work. From their union, Sleipnir is born.

Sleipnir's role in Norse mythology extends beyond being Odin's mount. He is also involved in several significant myths, including the story where Odin rides him to Hel, the realm of the dead, to seek knowledge about the fate of his son, Baldur. Sleipnir's ability to move between worlds highlights his status as a liminal figure, capable of traversing the boundaries that separate the realms of gods, humans, and the dead.

Nidhogg

Nidhogg, sometimes spelled Níðhöggr, is a formidable creature in Norse mythology, known primarily as a malicious dragon or serpent. Nidhogg resides in Niflheim, the lowest of the nine worlds, beneath the roots of Yggdrasil, the great world tree that connects all of the realms in Norse cosmology. The creature's name translates roughly to "malice striker" or "he who strikes with malice," reflecting its destructive nature.

Nidhogg's primary role in the mythology is as a force of decay and destruction. It continuously gnaws at the root of Yggdrasil, threatening the stability of the cosmic tree. In addition to its role with Yggdrasil, Nidhogg is also said to feed on the corpses of the dead. This gruesome trait places Nidhogg among the most feared creatures in Norse mythology, a symbol of death and decay.

Nidhogg's interactions with Ratatoskr, the squirrel who runs up and down Yggdrasil carrying messages, adds another layer to its character. Ratatoskr conveys insults between Nidhogg and an unnamed eagle that resides at the top of Yggdrasil, symbolizing the ongoing strife within the world tree and the constant tension between opposing forces in the cosmos.

Fafnir

Fafnir is a notable character in Norse mythology, originally a dwarf who transforms into a fearsome and avaricious dragon. His story is primarily recounted in the Volsunga Saga and the Poetic Edda, where he serves as a potent symbol of greed and the corrupting influence of wealth.

Fafnir's tale begins as a dwarf, son of the dwarf king Hreidmar. He and his family come into possession of a massive hoard of gold and a cursed ring, which were compensation from the god Odin for the killing of their brother, Otr, who could transform into an otter. The gold is cursed by Andvari, from whom it was taken, ensuring it would bring death and destruction to whoever possesses it. Driven by greed and the curse, Fafnir kills his father to gain sole possession of the treasure. He then takes the treasure to a remote heath and transforms into a dragon, a form that better suits his new, greedy and solitary nature.

Fafnir's transformation into a dragon signifies his complete succumbing to the greed and malevolence brought on by the cursed treasure. His fearsome presence on the heath, guarding his hoard, becomes widely known. Fafnir's story reaches its climax when Sigurd, the legendary hero, is guided by the dwarf Regin (Fafnir's brother) to slay the dragon. Sigurd digs a pit, lies in wait, and fatally stabs Fafnir as he crawls over the pit to reach a water source. Before he dies, Fafnir speaks to Sigurd, warning him of the curse of the gold and the treachery of Regin.

Valkyries

Brynhildr

Brynhildr, also known as Brunhild, is a complex and prominent figure in Norse mythology, often portrayed as a valkyrie and a shieldmaiden. Her story is most famously recounted in the Volsunga Saga and the Poetic Edda, as well as in Richard Wagner's opera cycle, "Der Ring des Nibelungen." Brynhildr is a character of great strength, honor, and tragic destiny, playing a pivotal role in the saga's narrative.

As a valkyrie, Brynhildr serves Odin, choosing those who will die in battle and those who will be granted victory. In one version of her story, after disobeying Odin's orders in a battle, she is punished by being stripped of her valkyrie status and condemned to live as a mortal woman. Odin places her in a remote castle, surrounded by a ring of fire, decreeing that only a hero who dares to brave the flames can awaken and marry her.

Sigurd, the saga's central hero, enters Brynhildr's story when he rides through the flames, awakens her with a kiss, and promises to return for her. However, due to deceptions and a potion-induced forgetfulness, Sigurd becomes betrothed to Gudrun, and Brynhildr is wed to Gunnar, Sigurd's comrade. Eventually, the truth of Sigurd's initial betrothal and love for Brynhildr is revealed, leading to a tragic series of events. Brynhildr, feeling betrayed and dishonored, instigates Sigurd's murder. Overcome with grief and guilt, she ultimately takes her own life at Sigurd's funeral pyre.

Gunnr, Rota, and Skuld

Gunnr, Rota, and Skuld are figures from Norse mythology, known as Valkyries. Valkyries, in Norse myth, are female figures who serve Odin, the chief of the Aesir gods. Their primary role is to choose the most heroic of those who have died in battle and to bring them to Valhalla, Odin's hall in Asgard, where they become Einherjar. This task is significant, as these warriors are to fight alongside the gods during Ragnarök, the prophesied end of the world.

Gunnr, Rota, and Skuld are among the more prominent Valkyries mentioned in the myths. While specific details about each of them are sparse, their roles are emblematic of the Valkyries' functions. Gunnr and Rota, along with Skuld, who is sometimes also depicted as a Norn (a being that determines fate), are said to wield considerable influence over the course of battles, selecting who will die and who will achieve glory. This selection process is not just a matter of choosing the slain but also involves determining the outcomes of conflicts.

Dwarves

Brokk and Sindri

Brokk and Sindri, also known as Eitri, are renowned dwarf brothers in Norse mythology, famed for their unparalleled skills in craftsmanship and metalworking. They play a crucial role in the mythological narratives, particularly in the tales that involve the creation of some of the gods' most significant and powerful artifacts.

The most famous story involving Brokk and Sindri is recounted in the Prose Edda, where they engage in a bet with Loki, the trickster god. Loki wagers his head that the brothers cannot create three objects superior to the ones made by the sons of Ivaldi (another group of skilled dwarf craftsmen). Accepting the challenge, Sindri and Brokk set to work in their forge. Sindri, the master craftsman, creates three magical items: Gullinbursti, a boar with bristles that glow in the dark; Draupnir, a golden ring that multiplies itself every ninth night; and Mjolnir, the mighty hammer of Thor. Despite Loki's attempts to sabotage their work, the brothers successfully complete the items, each imbued with magical properties. Mjolnir, in particular, becomes one of the most iconic and powerful objects in Norse mythology.

Dvalin

Dvalin is a figure from Norse mythology, known primarily as a dwarf. Dwarves in Norse myth are beings associated with great wisdom, craftsmanship, and the underground world. While Dvalin is not as prominently featured as some other characters in the myths, he is nonetheless an important figure, particularly in the context of dwarven lore and craftsmanship.

Dvalin's name appears in several Old Norse texts, and he is often linked to the creation of magical items and runes. In the Poetic Edda, Dvalin is mentioned as a leader among dwarves and as one who knows many runes. This association with runes underscores his role as a keeper of knowledge and magical skills, as runes in Norse mythology are not just a writing system but are also imbued with magical properties.

One significant mention of Dvalin is in the context of the creation of the Brisingamen, the famous necklace worn by the goddess Freyja. According to some versions of the myth, Dvalin is one of the dwarves responsible for forging this magnificent and magical piece, which further emphasizes his skill and artistry.

Alvis

Alvis ("All-Wise" or "All-Knowing") is a character from Norse mythology, notable primarily for his role in a tale that centers around knowledge, cunning, and the power of words. He is depicted as a dwarf, a being known in Norse myth for their exceptional skills in craftsmanship and deep wisdom.

Alvis's story is chiefly recounted in the poetic work "Alvissmal" ("The Words of Alvis"), found in the Poetic Edda. In this tale, Alvis comes to Asgard, the realm of the gods, to claim the hand of Thor's daughter, Thrud, whom he has been promised in marriage. Thor, however, is not inclined to let his daughter marry a dwarf and decides to prevent the union. To do this, he engages Alvis in a contest of wisdom.

Thor challenges Alvis to prove his intelligence by answering a series of questions about the cosmos. These questions cover various aspects of the Norse universe, including the realms of the gods, giants, and humans, and aspects of nature and the cosmos. Alvis answers all the questions skillfully, showcasing his vast knowledge. However, Thor's true intention is to delay Alvis until sunrise, as dwarves turn to stone in daylight. As Alvis completes his answers, the sun rises, and he is petrified by the sunlight, thus preventing the marriage.

Elves

The Dökkálfar

In Norse mythology, the Dökkálfar, often translated as "Dark Elves" or "Black Elves," are a group of beings whose exact nature and role are somewhat ambiguous and subject to different interpretations. The term "Dökkálfar" appears in the Prose Edda, written by Snorri Sturluson, where they are mentioned briefly and contrasted with the Ljósálfar, or "Light Elves."

The Dökkálfar are often thought to reside in Svartalfheim, one of the Nine Worlds in Norse cosmology, which is sometimes equated with Nidavellir, the realm of the dwarves. This association has led to some confusion and overlap in the roles and characteristics attributed to the Dökkálfar and dwarves.

While dwarves are well-known in Norse myth for their skill in craftsmanship and their connection to the earth, the exact nature of the Dökkálfar is less clear. They are often depicted as beings who dwell in dark or underground places and may possess magical abilities or attributes akin to those ascribed to traditional elves.

The Dökkálfar are rarely the central figures in Norse mythological stories and are mentioned only in passing in the primary sources. As such, much of their characteristics and stories are left to speculation and interpretation.

The Ljósálfar

In Norse mythology, the Ljósálfar, or "Light Elves," are celestial beings associated with light and purity. They stand in contrast to the Dökkálfar, or "Dark Elves," who are associated with darkness and the underground. The Ljósálfar are mentioned in the Prose Edda, written by Snorri Sturluson, where they are described as more beautiful to behold than the sun.

The Ljósálfar are believed to reside in Alfheim, one of the Nine Worlds, which is governed by the god Freyr. Unlike the Dökkálfar, who dwell in darkness, the Light Elves inhabit a bright and shining realm, often conceptualized as a place of beauty and radiance. Their characteristics and activities are not extensively detailed in the surviving Norse texts, leading to much of their nature and stories being open to interpretation.

Other Characters

Hel

Hel, in Norse mythology, is both a place and a personification of the realm of the dead. She is a significant figure, known as the ruler of the underworld, also called Hel. As a deity, Hel is often described as a daughter of Loki, the trickster god, and the giantess Angrboda, making her part of a family that includes the wolf Fenrir and the serpent Jormungandr, both of whom play significant roles in Norse cosmology.

Hel's domain, also named Hel, is where those who did not die in battle but of illness or old age go upon their death. Unlike Valhalla, Odin's hall where warriors slain in combat are taken by the Valkyries, Hel's realm is often depicted as a grim and dreary place. However, it should be noted that the Norse concept of the afterlife was not strictly binary; Hel's realm was not necessarily seen as a place of punishment but rather as a continuation of existence in another form.

In the mythological narratives, Hel is assigned her role by Odin. She is given authority over the nine worlds to govern those who enter her realm. Hel is often described as being half-living and half-dead, with a grim and stern appearance, embodying the duality of life and death. Her demeanor is typically impassive and implacable, reflecting her role as a dispassionate and unyielding ruler of the dead.

Sigurd

Sigurd, also known as Siegfried in some Germanic legends, is a legendary hero in Norse mythology, central to the Volsunga Saga and the Poetic Edda. His tale is one of heroism, love, betrayal, and tragedy, making him one of the most prominent figures in Norse legend.

Sigurd is the son of Sigmund, a great warrior, and Hjordis, and is born after his father's death in battle. Raised by Regin, a crafty dwarf, Sigurd is told of a great treasure, the hoard of the dragon Fafnir. Regin, desiring the treasure for himself, manipulates Sigurd into slaying Fafnir. Before confronting the dragon, Sigurd acquires the legendary sword Gram, reforged from the shattered pieces of his father's sword. With Gram, Sigurd kills Fafnir, becoming one of the most renowned dragon slayers in mythological lore.

Following the dragon's death, Sigurd is advised by the Odin-disguised bird to eat Fafnir's heart and bathe in his blood, granting him the ability to understand the language of birds. The birds warn Sigurd of Regin's treachery, leading Sigurd to kill Regin and take the hoard for himself. Amongst the hoard, he finds the cursed ring Andvaranaut, which brings misfortune to all its bearers.

Sigurd's most famous romantic involvement is with Brynhildr, a valkyrie. After awakening her from an enchanted sleep, they fall in love and promise to marry. However, due to deception and a magic potion, Sigurd marries Gudrun instead. This tangled web of love and betrayal ultimately leads to Sigurd's death, orchestrated by Gudrun's brother, Gunnar, and Brynhildr's subsequent suicide.

Sigurd's character is emblematic of the archetypal hero in Norse mythology. His life is marked by extraordinary feats, from slaying a fearsome dragon to obtaining cursed treasure. His story is not only a tale of bravery and strength but also of the complexities of fate, love, and honor.

Mimir

Mimir is a wise and enigmatic figure in Norse mythology, renowned for his knowledge and understanding. His name, often interpreted as "the rememberer" or "the wise one," reflects his role as a being of great wisdom. Mimir is not a god but rather a being who possesses profound knowledge and insight.

One of Mimir's most significant roles in Norse mythology is his association with the Well of Mimir, located beneath one of the roots of Yggdrasil, the world tree. This well is a source of deep wisdom and knowledge, and drinking from its waters grants enlightenment and understanding. Odin, the chief of the Aesir gods, seeks the water of this well in his quest for wisdom. Mimir, who guards the well, allows Odin to drink from it but demands a high price: one of Odin's eyes. This sacrifice by Odin is symbolic of his relentless pursuit of knowledge and the cost that often accompanies such a quest.

Mimir himself comes into prominence in the tales during the war between the Aesir and Vanir gods. Following the war, the gods exchange hostages as a peace gesture, and Mimir is sent to the Aesir. However, the Aesir are unable to understand or appreciate Mimir's wisdom, and he is eventually beheaded during a conflict. Odin, valuing Mimir's wisdom, preserves his head with magic and herbs, allowing Mimir to continue imparting knowledge and counsel to him.

Huginn and Muninn

Huginn and Muninn are a pair of ravens, closely associated with Odin, the chief of the Aesir gods. Their names translate to "Thought" (Huginn) and "Memory" (Muninn), symbolizing mental faculties that are crucial to wisdom and understanding.

As Odin's companions, they play a unique role in his quest for knowledge and his governance of the Norse cosmos.

Each day, Huginn and Muninn fly across the nine worlds, observing events and gathering information. At the end of the day, they return to Odin and whisper into his ears all that they have seen and heard. This daily ritual allows Odin to keep abreast of many happenings throughout the realms, even those far from his sight in Asgard. The ravens' ability to traverse the worlds reflects Odin's far-reaching quest for knowledge and his desire to oversee and understand all aspects of the universe.

Geri and Freki

Geri and Freki are two wolves, known for their close association with Odin. Their names roughly translate to "the ravenous" or "greedy one," reflecting their roles as Odin's loyal companions. In Norse myth, wolves are often symbols of strength, loyalty, and ferocity, and Geri and Freki embody these characteristics as constant companions to Odin.

According to the myths, Odin feeds Geri and Freki with his own food at the table in Valhalla, where the slain warriors, known as the Einherjar, feast. Despite the abundant food in Valhalla, Odin himself consumes only wine; the sustenance for his body comes from the wisdom and knowledge he gains.

Geri and Freki are more than just Odin's pets; they are also his companions in battles and his protectors. They are often depicted sitting beside him on his throne or accompanying him on the battlefield.

The Norns (Urd, Verdandi, Skuld)

The Norns are powerful female beings who play a crucial role in determining the course of destiny for both gods and men. They are often likened to the Fates in Greek mythology. The three primary Norns are Urd (representing the past), Verdandi (the present), and Skuld (the future). Their names can be translated respectively as "What Once Was," "What Is Coming into Being," and "What Shall Be."

The Norns reside by the well of Urd, located beneath one of the roots of Yggdrasil, the world tree that connects all the realms of the Norse cosmos. Here, they tend to the tree and weave the threads of fate. The Norns draw water from the well and pour it, along with sacred mud, over Yggdrasil's roots to prevent it from decaying. This act is crucial to maintaining the health and stability of the cosmic tree, and by extension, the entire cosmos.

The Norns' primary function, however, is to determine the fates of beings. They weave the threads of life, deciding the destinies of all beings from the moment of their birth to their death. This weaving is not just a passive recording of what will happen; it is an active shaping of events and outcomes. While the gods have significant power in Norse mythology, they are also subject to the Norns' decrees, illustrating the inescapable nature of fate and destiny.

Chapter 3: Creation Myth

In the beginning of Norse mythology, there existed a great void known as Ginnungagap, a vast, primordial chasm that separated the realms of intense heat and cold – Muspelheim, the land of fire, and Niflheim, the land of ice. Muspelheim, to the south, was ablaze with licking flames and smoldering sparks, while to the north, Niflheim was bitterly cold, covered in ice and frost. Between these two extremes was Ginnungagap, an empty space waiting to be filled.

In this expanse of nothingness, the hot air from Muspelheim met the cold air from Niflheim, causing the ice to thaw and drip. From these melting ice droplets emerged Ymir, the first of the ancient beings known as the Jotnar, or giants. Ymir was a hermaphroditic being and the progenitor of the race of frost giants. As he slept, more beings began to emerge from his body: a male and a female grew from his armpits, and his legs produced a six-headed son. These beings were the ancestors of the frost giants.

Alongside Ymir, the ice also gave birth to a cow named Audhumla. Audhumla nourished Ymir with her milk, and as she licked the salty ice blocks, a figure began to emerge. Over the course of three days, she uncovered a man named Buri. Buri was strong and handsome, and from him descended the line of gods. Buri fathered a son named Bor, who married Bestla, a giantess. Together, Bor and Bestla had three sons: Odin, Vili, and Ve.

These three brothers were powerful and wise, and they would come to play a pivotal role in shaping the cosmos. It was they who first confronted the untamed chaos of the world as it was. The brothers saw the potential in the yawning void of Ginnungagap and the raw, elemental forces at play in Muspelheim and Niflheim. They understood that from these primal elements, a new and ordered world could be forged.

The most significant act of Odin and his brothers was their confrontation with the giant Ymir. Ymir, being the progenitor of the frost giants, represented the chaotic and untamed forces of the old world. The brothers challenged and ultimately slew Ymir, marking a turning point in the mythic history. The death of Ymir was a transformative event, for from his body, the brothers fashioned the world. His flesh became the earth, his blood formed the seas and rivers, his bones were transformed into mountains, and his skull, held aloft by four dwarfs named Nordri, Sudri, Austri, and Vestri, became the sky. His brains were scattered across the sky as clouds, and from his eyebrows, the brothers built Midgard, the realm of humans.

With the physical structure of the world established, the brothers set about populating it. They found two tree trunks and from them, they created the first human beings. Odin gave them breath and life, Vili offered them intelligence and movement, and Ve provided them with senses, speech, and appearance. These first humans were named Ask and Embla, and Midgard became their dwelling place.

The creation of the world and the first humans set the stage for the establishment of a cosmic order. With the physical realms in place, the Norse cosmos took on a more structured form.

At the heart of this new order was Asgard, the realm of the gods, a magnificent fortress built by the Aesir to protect themselves from the giants. Asgard was connected to Midgard, the world of humans, by Bifrost, the rainbow bridge, which was both a link and a barrier between gods and mortals. The cosmic order was further anchored by Yggdrasil, the World Tree, a colossal ash tree that spanned the cosmos. Its branches extended into the nine different realms, which are as follows:

Asgard: The realm of the Aesir gods, including Odin, Thor, and Frigg. Asgard is a fortified realm where the gods reside and hold court.

Midgard: The realm of humans. It's considered the central realm where human beings live. In Norse cosmology, it's located in the middle of Yggdrasil and is surrounded by a vast ocean that is impassable.

Jotunheim (also known as Jotunheimar): The land of the giants, or Jotnar. It's a place of wilderness and untamed landscapes, often depicted as a realm of rock and ice, and it's here that the giants, who are often in conflict with the Aesir gods, reside.

Vanaheim: The home of the Vanir gods, a group of deities associated with fertility, prosperity, and foresight.

Alfheim: The realm of the Light Elves. In Norse mythology, elves are considered to be luminous beings who are "fairer than the sun to look at."

Svartalfheim (also known as Nidavellir): The realm of the Dwarves. Dwarves in Norse mythology are skilled craftsmen and are responsible for forging many of the gods' powerful weapons and tools.

Niflheim: Often associated with ice and cold, Niflheim is one of the first two realms to exist. It's a place of darkness and mist.

Muspelheim: A realm of fire and heat, Muspelheim is home to fire giants and demons. It's ruled by Surtr, a fearsome giant who, according to prophecy, will play a major role during Ragnarok.

Helheim: The realm of the dead, overseen by the goddess Hel. It's a destination for those who did not die in battle but of sickness or old age. Helheim is located withing the realm of Niflheim and is often depicted as a grim and cold place, contrasting with the heroic afterlife of Valhalla.

Chapter 4: The Aesir-Vanir War

In the ancient times of Norse mythology, there existed two divine tribes: the Aesir and the Vanir. The Aesir, gods of power and warfare, resided in Asgard and were led by the all-wise Odin. Their counterparts, the Vanir, associated with fertility, wisdom, and the ability to foresee the future, dwelled in the lush realm of Vanaheim. Among the Vanir were Njord and his children, Freyr and Freyja, deities of great esteem and power.

Tensions between these two tribes had been simmering for ages, but the fuse was lit with the arrival of the Vanir goddess Freyja in Asgard. Freyja, a master of the arcane arts of seidr, initially received a warm welcome. However, her prowess in magic, coupled with her wealth, soon kindled envy and fear among the Aesir. Unable to contain their trepidation and greed, the Aesir resolved to eliminate this perceived threat. In an act of aggression, they attempted to incinerate Freyja. Remarkably, each time they burned her, she was reborn from the ashes, more powerful than before.

In some versions of Norse mythology, the catalyst for the Aesir-Vanir War is not Freyja but a mysterious and enigmatic figure named Gullveig. Just as in the versions that suggest Freyja was the one burned by the Aesir, Gullveig's mistreatment at the hands of the Aesir ignited the fury of the Vanir. Whether she was one of them or simply a catalyst for the conflict, her story symbolizes the tension and misunderstanding between the two tribes of gods.

This affront did not go unnoticed by the Vanir. Outraged by the harm inflicted upon one of their kin, they declared war on the Aesir, marking the beginning of a catastrophic conflict that would reshape the divine world.

The war that ensued was unlike any other. The Aesir, renowned for their martial might, clashed with the Vanir, who wielded their profound magical abilities with precision. The battlefield was a spectacle of brute strength against enchanting sorcery. Despite the ferocity and valor displayed by both sides, a clear victor did not emerge. The prolonged struggle drained both tribes, and the once invincible Aesir and the indomitable Vanir realized the futility of their war.

In time, weariness paved the way for wisdom. Leaders from both sides convened, seeking an end to the bloodshed. A truce was proposed, one that required a profound act of trust: an exchange of hostages. From the Vanir, Njord and his children, Freyr and Freyja, were sent to Asgard. In return, the Aesir sent Honir, a figure of imposing stature and demeanor, and Mimir, a being of unparalleled wisdom, to Vanaheim.

However, peace came with its own tribulations. The Vanir soon discovered that Honir's wisdom was contingent on Mimir's counsel. Feeling deceived, they retaliated by beheading Mimir and sending his head back to Asgard. Odin, recognizing the value of Mimir's wisdom, preserved his head with enchantments, allowing Mimir to continue offering his invaluable advice.

The end of the war heralded a new era in the realms of the divine. The integration of the Vanir into Asgard brought with it new beliefs, practices, and a harmonious balance between once disparate powers. Freyja introduced the Aesir to her magical arts, while Freyr and Njord shared their deep connection with the earth and seas.

Thus, the Aesir-Vanir War, while born from conflict, ultimately wove together the fabric of the divine realms, enriching Norse mythology with tales of unity, resilience, and the blending of diverse strengths.

Chapter 5: The Binding of Fenrir

The story of the binding of Fenrir is a profound and captivating tale, rich in symbolism and dramatic imagery.

Born of the trickster god Loki and the giantess Angrboda, Fenrir was no ordinary wolf. His size and strength grew exponentially, outpacing all creatures in the realms. The gods, witnessing his monstrous growth, began to fear what havoc he might wreak upon the worlds, especially after a prophecy foretold that Fenrir would play a crucial role in Ragnarök, the end of the world.

The gods decided that Fenrir must be contained. They invited him to Asgard, the realm of the gods, under the guise of a test of his strength. Fenrir, proud and fearless, accepted. The first chain they presented to him, named Laeding, was robust and thick. Fenrir, assessing it, allowed himself to be bound, knowing he could break free. With a mere flex of his mighty muscles, Fenrir shattered the chain, much to the gods' dismay.

Undeterred, the gods forged a second, stronger chain, named Dromi. They approached Fenrir again, praising his strength and proposing another challenge. Fenrir, seeing the heavier chain, grew suspicious but agreed once more. Yet again, with a mighty heave, he broke free, proving his unparalleled strength. The gods' worry deepened, for they knew that if they could not bind Fenrir, he would indeed be a grave threat in times to come.

The gods turned to the dwarves, the most skilled smiths in all the realms. They requested a fetter that was unbreakable. The dwarves, using their mystical skills and secret ingredients, forged Gleipnir. Unlike the previous chains, Gleipnir was deceptively slender and soft, crafted from six mythical ingredients: the sound of a cat's footfall, the beard of a woman, the roots of a mountain, the sinews of a bear, the breath of a fish, and the spittle of a bird.

This time, when the gods approached Fenrir with Gleipnir, the wolf grew deeply suspicious. He sensed the magic in the fetter and understood that this was no ordinary challenge. He agreed to let himself be bound by it, but on one condition – that one of the gods place their hand in his mouth as a pledge of good faith. The gods hesitated, knowing the peril they faced. Finally, Tyr, the god of war and justice, stepped forward. He placed his hand in Fenrir's mighty jaws as the other gods bound the wolf.

When Fenrir found that he could not break free from Gleipnir, he understood he had been tricked. In his rage, he bit off Tyr's hand. The gods, relieved that Fenrir was finally contained, took him to a desolate place. There, they fastened Gleipnir to a great boulder and thrust a sword into Fenrir's jaws to keep them open, from which saliva flowed, forming a river. There Fenrir would remain bound until the events of Ragnarök, where it was prophesized that he would break free and seek his vengeance upon the gods.

Chapter 6: The Theft of Thor's Hammer

In the realm of Asgard, where the Aesir gods dwelt, there occurred an incident most unsettling. Thor, the god of thunder, known for his immense strength and valor, awoke one morning to find his most prized possession, the mighty hammer Mjolnir, missing. This hammer, a symbol of Thor's power, was also a vital safeguard for the gods against the giants.

Frantic, Thor searched his dwelling, only to find the hammer nowhere. He sought the help of Loki, the god of mischief, suspecting foul play. Loki, with his cunning mind and ability to shape-shift, was often the one to navigate the delicate matters of the gods.

Their first suspicion fell upon the giants, known enemies of the Aesir gods. Loki borrowed Freyja's falcon cloak, which granted the power of flight, and flew to Jotunheim, the land of the giants. There, he encountered Thrym, the king of the giants, who proudly admitted to stealing Mjolnir. He had hidden it deep beneath the earth and declared he would return it only in exchange for Freyja as his bride.

Loki returned to Asgard with this news. Freyja, outraged at the proposal, steadfastly refused. The gods convened to find a solution, and Heimdall, the ever-watchful guardian of the Bifrost Bridge, suggested a daring plan. Thor, he proposed, should disguise himself as Freyja and go to Jotunheim to retrieve Mjolnir.

Reluctantly, Thor agreed. Dressed in bridal garments, complete with a veil and jewels, and accompanied by Loki disguised as his bridesmaid, Thor set off to Jotunheim. The giants, fooled by their disguises, welcomed them with a grand feast. Thrym, enchanted by the prospect of marrying Freyja, did not recognize the mighty Thor beneath the bridal veil.

The feast was a grand affair, with tables laden with the finest foods and drinks the giants could muster. Roasted meats of all kinds, huge loaves of bread, and barrels of mead were arrayed for the guests. The giants, known for their enormous appetites, expected their guests to partake heartily in the feast.

However, Thor, hidden beneath his bridal veil and feminine disguise, was not one to hold back his immense appetite. To the astonishment of the giants, 'Freyja' began to eat voraciously. Thor consumed an entire ox, eight salmon, and all the delicacies prepared for the women, not to mention the vast quantities of mead he drank.

Thrym, the giant king, watched in amazement and alarm. Never had he seen a woman eat and drink so much. Loki, quick to maintain their ruse, explained that 'Freyja' had been so lovesick for Thrym that she had not eaten for eight days and nights, which the giants found reasonable and were thus reassured.

As the feast continued, Thrym, driven by his desire to see his bride, lifted the veil to steal a kiss. He was startled to see the glaring eyes of Thor, fierce and intimidating, staring back at him. Loki, ever the smooth talker, explained that 'Freyja' had not slept for eight nights in her excitement for the wedding, which accounted for her fiery eyes.

Thrym, eager to impress his bride-to-be, brought out Mjolnir to bless the marriage. The moment Thor saw his hammer, his rage and thirst for revenge could not be contained. He cast off his disguise, seized Mjolnir, and with the power of thunder and lightning at his command, unleashed his fury upon the giants.

Loki, quick to join the fray, helped Thor in the ensuing battle. Together, they fought fiercely, defeating Thrym and the giants, ensuring the safety of Asgard. With Mjolnir back in his possession, Thor's power was restored, and the balance between the gods and giants was maintained.

Their return to Asgard was marked by laughter and relief. The gods reveled in Thor's success and the clever ruse that had outwitted the giants. This tale, recounted with mirth and awe in the halls of Asgard, became a legendary account of cunning overcoming brute force, and the unbreakable spirit of the gods in the face of adversity.

Chapter 7: Odin and the Mead of Poetry

In the earliest of days, when the world itself was a tapestry of new stories and ancient magic, there existed a substance of unparalleled potency known as the Mead of Poetry. This was no ordinary mead, for it had the miraculous ability to bestow upon any who drank it the gift of poetry and wisdom. The mead's origin lay in tragedy and cunning, for it was crafted from the blood of Kvasir.

Kvasir, born from the saliva of the Aesir and Vanir gods, was a being of such profound wisdom that there was no question he could not answer. He roamed the realms, sharing his knowledge. However, his journey of enlightenment came to an abrupt and dark end. He was invited to the dwelling of two dwarves, Fjalar and Galar. These dwarves, envious and sly, murdered Kvasir, seeking to claim his wisdom for themselves. They mixed his blood with honey, thus creating the Mead of Poetry, a brew containing all of Kvasir's vast knowledge.

The dwarves' malevolence did not end with Kvasir. They soon played a role in the death of a giant named Gilling and his wife, leading to a vengeful chain of events. The giant's son, Suttung, enraged by the murder of his parents, captured the dwarves and demanded reparation. The dwarves offered the Mead of Poetry as a settlement, and Suttung, recognizing its value, agreed. He hid the mead deep within a mountain, guarded by his daughter Gunnlod, ensuring its safety and secrecy.

Odin, the Allfather and chief of the Aesir, heard tales of this mystical mead. His thirst for wisdom and power was unquenchable, and the lure of the Mead of Poetry was irresistible. He resolved to acquire it by any means necessary. Disguising himself as a traveler named Bolverk, he ventured toward the realm of the giants.

On his journey, Odin encountered nine servants of Baugi, Suttung's brother, who were laboriously working in the fields. Odin offered them the use of his whetstone to sharpen their scythes. The tool worked so miraculously well that each servant desired it for themselves, leading to a violent quarrel that resulted in their mutual destruction. Odin then approached Baugi, offering to undertake the work of the nine men, but with a singular condition – he demanded a taste of the Mead of Poetry as his payment.

Baugi, ignorant of Bolverk's true identity and the fate of his servants, agreed to the deal, albeit expressing his powerlessness in accessing the mead guarded by his brother Suttung. At the close of the harvest season, Baugi confessed his inability to procure the mead. Odin, ever resourceful, suggested a cunning plan. He presented Baugi with a drill, Rati, instructing him to bore a hole into the mountain where the mead was hidden.

After arduous efforts, a hole was made into the mountain. Odin, transforming himself into a serpent, slithered through this passage and found his way to where Gunnlod guarded the sacred mead. Returning to his godly form, he used his charm and guile to win Gunnlod's trust. He struck a deal with her: he would spend three nights with her, and in return, he would be allowed three sips of the Mead of Poetry.

Gunnlod, captivated by Odin's disguise and words, agreed to the arrangement. Over the course of three nights, Odin enchanted her with stories and promises. When the time came to drink the mead, Odin, in a display of his true intent and formidable power, consumed all the mead in just three enormous gulps, each gulp draining an entire vat.

Transforming once more, this time into an eagle, Odin soared towards Asgard, the mead safely within him. Suttung, upon realizing the deceit and theft, transformed into an eagle as well and gave chase. The chase was intense and perilous, spanning the skies between the realm of the giants and Asgard, the realm of the gods. Odin, burdened with the mead and just barely ahead, pushed himself to the limits of his divine strength to reach Asgard before Suttung could catch him.

As Odin approached Asgard, the other gods, aware of his plan, were prepared. They had set out containers in the courtyard of Asgard. Just as Odin reached the safety of Asgard, he regurgitated the Mead of Poetry into these containers.

However, in his haste, a small portion of the mead spilled out, accessible to anyone, giving rise to mediocre poets and scholars.

The exact fate of Suttung at this point varies slightly in different retellings of the myth. In some versions, as soon as Odin had safely returned the mead to Asgard, the gods were ready to defend their realm and Odin. In these accounts, Suttung, realizing he could not breach the stronghold of the gods, retreated, defeated and bereft of the mead.

In other versions, Suttung's pursuit leads to his demise. As he attempted to enter Asgard, he was either repelled by the gods and killed or simply could not overcome the fortifications of Asgard and fell to his death. Regardless of the version, the end result is the same: Suttung fails to retrieve the Mead of Poetry and Odin successfully brings it to the gods.

Odin's quest for the Mead of Poetry was not just a pursuit of a magical drink, but a reflection of his endless search for knowledge and power.

Chapter 8: The Fortification of Asgard

The Aesir gods came to the agreement that they needed to fortify Asgard, their celestial stronghold. The world was full of dangers, and a robust defense was necessary to protect the home of the gods.

It was during this time of planning and discussion that a mighty and enigmatic figure arrived in Asgard. He was a master builder, and he offered to erect an impregnable wall around Asgard, a wall so strong that it would keep out any intruder, be they giant, troll, or any other foe that threatened the gods. But his price was steep: he demanded the sun, the moon, and the hand of Freyja, the most beautiful of the goddesses, in marriage.

The gods, led by Odin, were wary of this stranger and his audacious demand. They deliberated long and hard, and finally, they proposed a counteroffer. The builder would receive his payment only if he managed to complete the wall within a single winter, and with no one's help but that of his horse, Svaðilfari. Confident that such a task was impossible, the gods felt secure in their bargain.

To their astonishment, the builder agreed, and the work began. The builder's horse, Svaðilfari, was no ordinary animal; it possessed immense strength and played a crucial role in the construction. As the days passed, the gods watched in disbelief as the wall neared completion at an astonishing pace. The builder, with Svaðilfari's help, was fulfilling his part of the bargain, much to the gods' dismay.

With only a few days left of winter, the wall was nearly complete. The gods, realizing that they would soon have to uphold their end of the bargain, panicked. Losing the sun and the moon would bring catastrophe to the world, and they could not bear to part with Freyja. They turned their anger and blame towards Loki, the trickster god, for he had been the one to suggest the builder's terms.

Loki, known for his cunning and resourcefulness, devised a plan to thwart the builder. He transformed himself into a mare and lured Svaðilfari away from his work. The absence of his horse greatly slowed the builder's progress. As winter's end approached, it became clear that the builder would not meet the deadline.

On the final day of winter, with the wall still incomplete, the builder's true identity was revealed – he was no mere mortal craftsman but a mountain giant in disguise.

The giant, upon realizing that he had been tricked and would not receive his payment, flew into a rage. He threatened to tear down the walls of Asgard and bring ruin to the realm of the gods. It was clear that a violent confrontation was inevitable.

Thor, never one to shy away from battle, especially against a giant, confronted the builder. The giant, confident in his own strength, prepared to fight. The standoff between Thor and the giant was tense, with the other gods watching, aware of the potential destruction this battle could bring to Asgard.

However, Thor, wielding Mjolnir, his fearsome hammer, was unmatched in combat. The hammer, a symbol of Thor's power and a weapon feared by all giants, was capable of tremendous destruction. With a single, mighty blow from Mjolnir, Thor struck the giant. The impact was so great that it instantly killed the giant, ending the threat to Asgard in one decisive action.

However, the consequences of Loki's interference were not yet fully realized. His escapade with Svaðilfari led to the birth of Sleipnir, an eight-legged horse, who would later become Odin's mighty steed.

Thus, the fortification of Asgard was completed, albeit through a series of unexpected and tumultuous events. This story, enshrined in the annals of Norse mythology, serves as a reminder of the gods' vulnerability and the unpredictable nature of deals with unknown entities.

Chapter 9: The Death of Baldur

The death of Baldur, one of the most poignant and tragic tales in Norse mythology, involves a complex web of fate, deception, and the inevitable march towards Ragnarök, the end of the world.

Baldur was the son of Odin and Frigg, and he was beloved by all in Asgard for his beauty, grace, and kindness. However, amidst this idyllic existence, a shadow of doom began to creep over Asgard, as Baldur started having ominous dreams of his own death. These dreams deeply troubled the gods, for they knew such visions often carried the weight of prophecy.

Frigg, his mother, heart heavy with fear for her son, resolved to protect him at all costs. She traveled across the world, from the highest heavens to the deepest seas, securing promises from every being, every object, and every force, that they would not harm Baldur. Stones, metals, woods, animals, even the elements themselves, swore oaths to Frigg that they would never be the cause of Baldur's demise. Satisfied with her efforts, Frigg returned to Asgard, confident that she had thwarted the dark fate foretold in Baldur's dreams.

But in the world of gods, nothing escapes the notice of Loki, the sly and cunning trickster. He discovered that in her exhaustive quest, Frigg had overlooked one seemingly insignificant plant:

the mistletoe, too young and frail, in her eyes, to cause any harm. Sensing an opportunity for mischief and chaos, Loki crafted a devious plan.

Meanwhile, in Asgard, the gods, assured of Baldur's invincibility, reveled in a new game. They would throw objects at Baldur, only to watch them bounce off harmlessly, their faces alight with laughter and joy. Baldur stood amidst them, a smile on his lips, as spears, stones, and arrows fell away, unable to touch the beloved god.

It was in this scene of merriment that Loki enacted his cruel plot. He approached Hodr, Baldur's blind brother, who stood aside, unable to partake in the festivities. With honeyed words, Loki offered to help Hodr join in, suggesting he too throw something at Baldur. He placed in Hodr's hand a dart made of mistletoe and guided his aim towards Baldur.

The mistletoe dart, the only object not sworn to avoid harming Baldur, flew through the air, guided by Loki's treacherous hand. It struck Baldur, piercing him through. The laughter died on the lips of the gods as Baldur collapsed, a look of surprise etched on his fair face. The brightest light in Asgard had been extinguished, and a heavy gloom settled over the realm.

The gods were stricken with grief, none more so than Odin and Frigg. Odin, the All-Father, knew too well that Baldur's death was a harbinger of the dreaded Ragnarok, the end of all things.

Frigg's heart was shattered, her efforts to protect her son all in vain. Amidst the sorrow, she spoke, her voice a mere whisper, asking if there was anyone who would venture into the cold depths of Hel to retrieve Baldur from the clutches of death.

Hermod, another of Odin's sons, stepped forward, his heart set on the perilous journey. He mounted Sleipnir, Odin's eight-legged steed, and rode hard and fast, down to the gates of Hel, the land of the dead.

In Helheim, Hermod pleaded before Hel, the ruler of the underworld, for Baldur's return. Hel, her gaze as cold as the realm she ruled, laid forth her condition: Baldur would be returned to the living if every creature, every object, every force in the universe wept for him. If all creation shared in the grief of the gods, then Baldur would be released from the realm of the dead.

Messengers were sent far and wide, and tears were shed for Baldur by all. From the mightiest giants to the smallest ants, from stones to stars, all wept for the fallen god. However, a single holdout shattered the collective effort: a giantess named Thokk, believed by many to be Loki in disguise, refused to shed a tear. "Let Hel keep what she has," she declared, and with those words, the fate of Baldur was sealed. He would remain in the realm of the dead, his light absent from the world until the dawn of Ragnarök.

Loki's role in Baldur's death was soon uncovered, and the gods captured the trickster. His punishment was severe: he was bound beneath the earth, a venomous serpent placed above him, its poison dripping endlessly onto his face. His wife, Sigyn, stayed by his side, catching the venom in a bowl, but whenever she left to empty it, the poison would strike Loki, causing him unbearable agony.

Thus, the death of Baldur, the brightest among the Aesir, marked the beginning of the end, the first in the chain of events that would lead to Ragnarök. In this tale of loss and betrayal, the gods of Asgard were reminded of the inexorable nature of fate and the inevitability of the prophesied end of their world.

Chapter 10: Ragnarök

After Baldur's death, a profound sense of doom settled over the gods. They knew that his demise was a significant omen, marking the beginning of the end. The immediate aftermath was marked by a period of mourning and despair, as the gods grappled with the inevitability of their fates.

The first major sign of the approaching Ragnarök was the onset of Fimbulwinter, a great and terrible winter that lasted three years with no summer in between. This harsh winter was to be the final winter of the world, a time of strife, conflict, and famine. Brothers would turn against brothers, and all moral bonds between men would break, leading to an age of lawlessness and chaos.

As Fimbulwinter ravaged the world, Loki, who had been bound by the gods as punishment for his role in Baldur's death, was finally freed from his bonds as they snapped, signaling the impending doom. With Loki free, the forces of chaos and destruction began to stir.

At the same time, the giants, long-standing enemies of the gods, mobilized for war. The fire giant Surtr led the fiery inhabitants of Muspelheim, wielding a flaming sword that shone brighter and hotter than the sun. From Jotunheim, the frost giants, led by Loki, prepared to march against Asgard.

Fenrir, the monstrous offspring of Loki and the giantess Angrboda, had been bound by the gods, for they feared his growing strength and ferocity. The gods had tricked him into being restrained with a magical ribbon, Gleipnir, forged of impossible things - the sound of a cat's footfall, the beard of a woman, the roots of a mountain, the sinews of a bear, the breath of a fish, and the spittle of a bird. Deceived and enraged, Fenrir lay bound on a desolate island, biding his time, his hatred for the gods growing with each passing moment.

As Ragnarök dawned, the earth trembled, and Fenrir's bonds shattered. With a roar that shook the very foundations of Yggdrasil, the World Tree, he broke free, his jaws gaping wide, threatening to devour everything in his path.

At the same time, Jormungandr, the Midgard Serpent, released his tail from his mouth and emerged from the depths of the sea, causing massive waves and flooding the land. The realms trembled as these monstrous beings unleashed their fury.

In Asgard, the gods prepared for the inevitable battle. Odin consulted the head of Mimir for wisdom, and the gods and their allies, the Einherjar, assembled their forces. The air was thick with tension, the sky alight with ominous signs.

Heimdall, the watchman of the gods, stood guard at the Bifrost bridge, the rainbow bridge connecting Asgard to Midgard. He was in possession of Gjallarhorn, a mighty horn whose blast was to signal the beginning of Ragnarök. As the enemies of the gods assembled and the signs of the end times became unmistakable, Heimdall blew Gjallarhorn with all his might, its sound echoing across all the worlds, calling the gods to battle.

As the first light of dawn touched the skies above Vigrid, the great plain where the fate of the cosmos was to be decided, an ominous rumble echoed through the realms. It was the sound of Fenrir, the monstrous wolf. His eyes, burning with hatred and madness, fixed upon Odin, the All-Father, the ruler of Asgard and the one who had ordered his imprisonment.

The gods, gathered in their might, looked upon this fearsome beast with a mix of awe and terror. Odin, atop his steed Sleipnir, clad in gleaming armor, knew that his destiny was at hand. The prophecy had foretold that he would fall to Fenrir, yet he rode forth, spear Gungnir in hand, resolved to face his fate with the valor befitting a king of gods.

The air was thick with tension as Fenrir lunged towards Odin. The All-Father thrust his spear with all his might, but Fenrir's massive jaws clamped down upon him. In one swift, dreadful moment, the wolf's teeth tore through divine flesh, and Odin, the wisest of all beings, was no more. His demise sent a wave of shock and despair through the ranks of the Aesir.

Meanwhile, Thor, the god of thunder, found his ancient nemesis in the roiling chaos of the battlefield. The Midgard Serpent,

Jormungandr, had emerged from the depths, its enormous body coiling and uncoiling, its venomous breath scorching the earth. Thor, wielding Mjolnir, his mighty hammer, charged at the serpent with a thunderous roar. The two titans clashed, lightning and venom filling the air. With a mighty blow, Thor crushed the serpent's head, but not without cost. As he staggered back, he was struck by Jormungandr's lethal venom. He took nine paces before he collapsed, succumbing to the poison.

Elsewhere on the battlefield, Freyr, the god of fertility, who had given away his magical sword, faced Surtr, the fearsome fire giant from Muspelheim. Surtr's flaming sword, bright as the sun, clashed with Freyr's antler. The battle was fierce, but without his sword, Freyr was at a disadvantage. Eventually, Surtr's blade found its mark, and Freyr fell, a victim to the flames that soon would consume the world.

Loki, the god of mischief, now a foe to the gods, engaged in combat with Heimdall, the guardian of the Bifrost. Their enmity ran deep, and their fight was one of both fury and desperation. They exchanged blow for blow, their weapons ringing out amidst the cacophony of battle. In the end, they dealt each other mortal wounds, fulfilling the destiny that had long been foretold for them.

Tyr, the one-handed god of war, confronted Garm, the hellhound that guarded the gates of Hel. Their battle was brutal and bloody, and though Tyr fought valiantly, he and the monstrous hound slew each other, adding to the growing number of casualties in this cataclysmic conflict.

As the battle raged, the world itself seemed to unravel. The fires of Surtr spread across the land, consuming gods, giants, and mortals alike. The seas boiled, the earth split apart, and the stars fell from the heavens. Chaos reigned as the prophesied end of all things came to pass.

As the flames of Surtr receded and the tumultuous seas calmed, the world of Ragnarök, scarred and reshaped by the cataclysm, lay in a profound stillness. The great battle had ceased, and with it, the old order of gods and men had passed into legend. The once mighty Yggdrasil, the World Tree, stood wounded yet enduring, its roots delving deep into the rejuvenated earth, its branches reaching into the cleansed skies.

In this new dawn, where the remnants of the old world met the promise of the new, a few beings emerged, destined to shape the future. Among the survivors were Vidar and Vali, the sons of Odin. Vidar, who had avenged his father's death by slaying Fenrir, stood tall and strong, a symbol of the enduring spirit of the Aesir. Vali, born in the shadows of impending doom, was now a beacon of hope in the renewed world.

Thor's sons, Modi and Magni, walked amidst the new green, carrying with them Mjolnir, the hammer of their father, a reminder of the thunder god's might and valor. They embodied the strength and courage that had defined the gods of old.

In a remarkable twist of fate, Baldur, the beloved god once slain by Loki's deceit, returned from the dead, accompanied by his brother Hodr. Their resurrection was a sign of the restoration of purity and light, long absent from the cosmos.

And in the sheltered grove of Hoddmimis Holt, two humans, Lif and Lifthrasir, emerged. Having survived the destruction by hiding within the mighty Yggdrasil, they were the hope of mankind, the seeds from which the human race would sprout anew.

The world they stepped into was a land reborn. It was as if the earth had been washed clean, the scars of the past erased by the trials of Ragnarök. The fields were lush and fertile, the air fresh and clear. It was an untouched world, free from the sorrows and shadows that had once shrouded the old realms.

In the aftermath, the surviving gods gathered in Idavoll, a field in Asgard that had withstood the end of days. Here, amidst the verdant fields, they spoke of the past, recounting tales of the fallen gods, of Odin's wisdom, Thor's bravery, and Loki's treachery. They found the golden game pieces that the Aesir had once played with, symbols of a time of innocence and joy, now a memory to cherish in the new world.

This new era was marked not by the conflict and strife that had defined the old world, but by a sense of harmony and potential. It was a time for new stories, for new legends to be born. The cycle of destruction and rebirth, so central to Norse cosmology, had turned once again. In the wake of Ragnarök, amidst the whispering leaves of Yggdrasil and the gentle rolling fields of Idavoll, the survivors stood at the dawn of a world reborn, ready to carve out their destinies in a land that promised endless possibilities.

Conclusion

As we close the pages of "Norse Mythology: A Collection of the Best Norse Myths," we step back from a journey through an ancient and mystical world that has unfurled its rich tapestry before us. This collection has not only narrated stories but has also offered a window into the Norse worldview, where every element of nature and every twist of fate is imbued with deeper meaning.

We began our exploration with an introduction to the formidable gods of the Aesir and Vanir in Chapter 1, delving into their origins, powers, and the intricate web of relationships that define the pantheon. In Chapter 2, we broadened our scope to the myriad other characters of Norse lore - the giants, valkyries, dwarves, and other mystical beings, each playing a pivotal role in the grand cosmic drama.

The Creation Myth, recounted in Chapter 3, brought us the extraordinary story of how the cosmos came into being, from the yawning void of Ginnungagap to the emergence of Yggdrasil, the world tree. The narrative of creation set the stage for the tales that followed, each steeped in symbolic meaning and reflective of the Norse understanding of the universe.

In Chapter 4, the Aesir-Vanir War provided a glimpse into the divine conflict and reconciliation, a saga that echoed themes of power, diplomacy, and unity. We witnessed the complexity of divine relationships and the nuanced portrayal of inter-tribal dynamics.

The Binding of Fenrir in Chapter 5 brought us face to face with the themes of prophecy, trust, and betrayal, as the gods dealt with the ominous destiny foretold for them. This tale led us into the intrigue and cunning that characterize many Norse myths.

In Chapter 6, we explored "The Theft of Thor's Hammer," a blend of action, humor, and cunning, showcasing the depth and versatility of these ancient narratives. The story was not just an action-packed adventure but also a commentary on the interplay of strength, wisdom, and deception.

Odin's quest for wisdom in "Odin and the Mead of Poetry" in Chapter 7 highlighted the value placed on knowledge and the sacrifices made in its pursuit. This story, rich in symbolism, emphasized the power of words and the origin of poetic inspiration.

The Fortification of Asgard in Chapter 8 narrated the gods' efforts in protecting their realm, a tale that combined themes of protection, trickery, and craftsmanship. It showed how even gods are not immune to threats and their constant struggle for security.

In Chapter 9, we delved into the poignant "Death of Baldur," a tale that embodies the themes of loss, prophecy, and the inescapable nature of fate. This chapter set the stage for the final destiny of the gods.

Finally, Chapter 10 brought us to the climax of Norse mythology - Ragnarök, the end of the world. This apocalyptic tale was not just about destruction, but also about the cycles of nature, renewal, and the enduring nature of life and hope.

In conclusion, "Norse Mythology: A Collection of the Best Norse Myths" has been a voyage across a spectrum of tales that are as diverse in their themes as they are rich in their storytelling. From the creation of the world to its ultimate end, these myths have offered insights into the Norse perspective on life, nature, and the divine. They have underscored the importance of valor, wisdom, loyalty, and the acceptance of fate. As we part with these tales, we carry with us not only the stories of gods and heroes but also the timeless wisdom embedded within them, relevant even in today's world.

I hope you have enjoyed this exploration into the world of Norse Mythology. If you would like to share your feedback, it is greatly appreciated if you could take a minute to leave us a review on Amazon. It really helps us to continue producing books that readers love!

And finally, if you liked this book, please keep an eye out for the other books in this series, also available for sale on Amazon as well as through many other online retailers. The other books in this series include:

- Roman Mythology: A Collection of the Best Roman Myths

- Greek Mythology: A Collection of the Best Greek Myths

- Egyptian Mythology: A Collection of the Best Egyptian Myths

- Celtic Mythology: A Collection of the Best Celtic Myths